Something Old

Recipe: <u>Squash Bread</u>

- 1 bowl milk
- 1 bowl squash
- 1 cup yeast
- 2/3 cup sugar
- 2/3 cup butter

Mix flour in the same as any bread. Bake in oven at 350F degrees for about 25 minutes or until brown. Enjoy!

Recipe: <u>Oatmeal Muffins</u>

- 1 cup oatmeal mush
- 1 cup water
- 2 cups milk
- 1 tsp butter
- ½ cake compressed yeast
- Pinch of salt
- Flour, enough to make batter

Add flour to make stiff batter, let rise over night. Bake in muffin rings at 350F degrees for about 15 minutes or until brown around edges. Enjoy!

Recipe: <u>Graham Wafers</u>

- 1 cup cream
- 3 cups graham flour
- Pinch of salt
- 1 tbs sugar
- milk

Mix ingredients. Add enough milk to make it thin. Enjoy!

Recipe: <u>Troy Pudding</u>

- 1 cup raisins
- 1 cup suet
- 1 cup molasses
- 1 cup milk
- 3 ½ cups flour
- 1 tsp baking soda

Stir all ingredients together. Boil for 3 hours. Serve with sweet sauce. Enjoy!

Recipe: <u>Election Cake</u>

- 23 ½ cups flour (7 lbs)
- 4 cups sugar (2 lbs)
- 6 sticks butter (1 ½ lbs)
- 7 eggs
- spice of choice

Mix well with warm milk. Bake at 350F degrees until brown around edges. Enjoy!

Recipe: <u>Cough Mixture</u>

- 2 oz gum Arabic
- 1 oz paregoric elixir
- 2 oz sugar candy
- 1 lemon, juiced
- 6 glasses hot water

Mix ingredients together. One glass to be taken three times a day at morning, noon and night.

Recipe: <u>Pancakes</u>

- 1 qt sweetened water
- 1 cup Indian meal
- ½ cup flour
- 1 tsp saleratus
- pinch of salt

Make stiff. Enjoy!

Recipe: <u>Sponge Cake</u>

- 1 cup flour
- 1 cup sugar
- 3 eggs
- ½ tsp baking soda
- 1 tsp cream of tartar
- 4 tbs water
- Lemon flavoring

Preheat oven to 350F degrees. Whisk eggs and sugar for 20 minutes. Sift flour and baking soda twice. Add all ingredients together and mix. Pour into 9 inch round pans. Bake for 30 minutes or until brown around edges. Enjoy!

Recipe: <u>Shingles</u>

- 1 cup sour milk
- 2 cups sugar
- 1 cup butter
- 1 tsp baking soda
- pinch of salt
- flour

Add ingredients together and mix. Roll out into flour until stiff. Bake at 350F degrees for 35 minutes or until golden brown. Enjoy!

Recipe: <u>Farmers Pork Cake</u>

- 1 lb of fat pork (finely chopped)
- 3 ½ cups brown sugar
- 1 ½ cups molasses
- 3 ½ cups sour milk
- 1 egg
- 4 tsp baking soda
- 1 ½ tsp cream of tartar
- 7 cups flour
- 2 tbs cloves
- 1 tbs cinnamon
- ½ tbs pepper
- 2 nutmegs
- 5 2/3 cups raisins
- 3 ¼ cups currants
- ½ citron

Mix the fruit with 1 cup flour. Enough for four large loaves. It will keep a year. Enjoy!

Recipe: <u>Hodge Podge</u>

- 4 qt chopped green tomatoes
- 1 qt chopped onions
- ½ cup + 2 tbs chopped green peppers
- ½ cup + 2 tbs salt

Put salt on tomatoes, let stand overnight. Drain. Add other ingredients. Cover with cold vinegar. Enjoy!

Recipe: <u>Mountain Dew Pudding</u>

- 4 crackers, rolled fine
- ½ pt milk
- Pinch of salt
- 2 eggs, separated
- ½ cup sugar
- ¼ tsp lemon extract

Mix crackers, milk and salt well. Pour into pan to bake for 20 minutes. Beat egg whites to a thick froth. Add sugar and lemon flavoring, gently fold in. Pour over top. Set in oven until browned. Enjoy!

Recipe: <u>Receipt for Colds</u>

- 1 lb liverwort
- 4 qts water
- ½ lb ball liquor ice
- ¼ lb loaf sugar
- ½ pint gin

Put liverwort in water and boil down to 1 qt liquid. Let cool until warm. Add the ball of liquor ice and sugar. When completely cooled, add gin. Dose half a large wine glass ½ hour before each meal. Enjoy!

Recipe: <u>Squash Muffins</u>

First day:

- 1 pt squash, strained
- ½ cup butter, melted
- ½ cup sugar
- ½ cup yeast
- 1 cup milk
- pinch of salt
- flour

Mix until batter is stiff and let rise overnight.

Second Day:

- 1 tsp baking soda
- 1 egg
- flour, just a little

Add baking soda, egg, and flour. Mix and bake in muffin pan at 350F degrees for 15 minutes or until golden brown. Enjoy!

APPETIZERS

Recipe: <u>Maply Appetizers</u>

- 1 – 13 ½ oz can pineapple chunks
- 2 – 8 oz pkg brown and serve sausage links
- 4 tsp corn starch
- ½ tsp salt
- ½ cup maple flavored syrup
- 1/3 cup water
- 1/3 cup vinegar
- 1 large green pepper, cut into ¾ inch squares
- ½ cup drained maraschino cherries

Drain pineapple, reserving liquid. Cut sausages in thirds crosswise. Brown sausage in skillet. Blend cornstarch, salt, reserved pineapple juice, maple syrup, water and vinegar together in a pan. Heat to boiling, stirring constantly. Add pineapple, sausage, pepper and cherries. Cook 5 minutes. Keep warm in chafing dish. Seer with cocktail picks. Enjoy!

Tasty for the Holidays.

Recipe: <u>Cheese Marbles</u>

- 2 cups cheddar cheese, grated
- ½ cup butter
- 1 cup flour
- 1/8 tsp salt

Blend cheese with butter then add flour and salt. Roll dough into balls the size of marbles. Bake on greased cookie sheet for 10 minutes at 350F degrees. Serve hot. Enjoy!

Recipe: <u>Cucumber Hor D'oeuvres</u>

- ½ package dry Italian dressing mix
- 1 pkg cream cheese
- mayonnaise, enough to make spreadable

Mix together. Spread mixture on small rounds of bread. Shake a pinch of dill on top for flavor. Enjoy!

Recipe: <u>Marinated Mushrooms</u>

- 1 lb button mushrooms
- 1 clove garlic (or 1/8 tsp garlic powder)
- 1 tsp salt
- 2 bay leaves
- 1 onion, thinly sliced
- 2 tbs catsup
- 1 lemon wedge
- 1 cup cider vinegar
- ¼ cup oil

Wash and simmer mushrooms for 5 minutes in salted water with a slice of lemon. Shake gently. Marinate at least 24 hours in refrigerator. Store in a covered jar. Enjoy!

PUNCH

Recipe: <u>Cranberry Punch</u>

- 2 cups undiluted orange juice
- 1 pt light rum OR pineapple juice
- 1 qt cranberry juice
- ½ cup sugar
- 1 qt ginger ale OR soda water

Mix together in punch bowl. Enjoy!

Recipe: <u>Tomato Bouillon</u>

- 1 large can tomato juice
- 4 cups water
- 4 chicken bouillon cubes
- ½ cup lemon juice
- Sugar, salt, celery salt to taste

Heat ingredients together, dissolving bouillon cubes. If tomato juice is too thick, add more water and 1 bouillon cube. Serve on cold day in place of coffee or tea. Enjoy!

Recipe: <u>Tomato Juice Cocktails</u>

- 2 qts tomato juice (fresh or canned)
- 3 tsp salt
- 3 tsp celery salt
- 1 tsp horseradish
- 3 tbs lemon juice
- 1/8 tsp Worcestershire sauce
- 1 tsp onion juice

Mix and serve chilled. Enjoy!

Recipe: <u>Hot Spiced Wine</u>

- 1 cup sugar
- 3 cups boiling water
- ½ lemon rind
- 18 cloves, whole
- 1 or more cinnamon sticks

Stir sugar into boiling water. Then add lemon rind, cloves and cinnamon sticks and boil for 15 minutes. Strain into top of double boiler. Add burgundy or claret and heat until hot. DO NOT BOIL. Enjoy!

SOUPS

Recipe: <u>Cream of Carrot Soup</u>

- 3 carrots, sliced
- 1 cup water
- 1 onion
- 1 bay leaf
- 1 tsp salt
- 1 ½ tbs butter
- 1 tsp ground pepper
- 1 cup hot milk
- ½ cup cream

Cover carrots and cook until tender. Rub through strainer and reserve water. Place water and carrots over heat. If mixture is too thick add more water. Add butter. Beat until thick and boiling. Just before serving add salt, pepper, milk and cream. Enjoy!

Recipe: <u>Appetizer Broccoli Soup</u>

- 2 - 10 oz pkg frozen broccoli, chopped
- 2 cans cream of mushroom soup
- 2 2/3 cups milk
- ½ cup dry white wine
- 4 tbs butter
- 1 tsp salt
- 1 tsp pepper
- 1 ½ tbs dried tarragon, crushed

In large saucepan cook broccoli as directed on package. Drain. Add soup, milk, wine, butter, salt, pepper, and tarragon. Heat, but do not boil. Serve and enjoy!

Serves 9

Recipe: <u>Curried Cream of Apple Soup</u>

- 1 stick butter
- 1 medium onion, sliced
- 4 large apples, peeled, cored and sliced (reserve some for garnish)
- 1 lg carrot, sliced
- 1 green pepper, seeded and finely chopped
- 1 celery stalk, sliced
- 2 cloves, whole
- 1-2 tsp curry powder
- 1 parsley sprig, minced
- Pinch of nutmeg
- 5 cups chicken broth
- 1 tsp salt
- 1 tsp pepper
- 1 cup whipping cream

Melt butter in a pan and sauté onion, carrots, pepper and celery for 10 minutes, or until soft. Stir in seasonings. Cover, reduce heat and simmer for 30 minutes. Remove from heat and stir in cream. Puree in blender. Serve hot or cold with garnish. Enjoy!

Recipe: <u>Salmon Chowder</u>

- 1 small onion
- 2 cups diced carrots
- 6 cups diced potatoes
- 6 cups water
- 1 can pink salmon
- 1 can evaporated milk
- 1 tsp salt
- 1 tsp pepper

Boil onion, carrots, and potatoes together until tender. Move to back range on stove. Add salmon, evaporated milk, salt and pepper. Let stand for 1 hour. Serve and enjoy!

Recipe: <u>Creamy Shrimp Mushroom Soup</u>

- 1 - 10 ½ oz can cream of mushroom soup
- 1 - 10 ½ oz can cream of asparagus soup
- ½ cup sherry
- 1 2/3 cups milk
- 1 cup cooked shrimp, cut into halves
- Soup can of water

In medium saucepan combine undiluted soups. Gradually add soup can of water, sherry and milk. Heat to boiling point. Add shrimp. Stir occasionally. Enjoy!

Serves 8

Recipe: <u>Zucchini Sour Cream Soup</u>

- 2 ½ lbs zucchini, sliced
- 1/3 stick butter
- 1 ½ large onions, sliced thin
- 5 ½ cups water
- 3 bouillon cubes
- 2 ½ cups milk
- ½ tbs salt
- Pinch of pepper
- Pinch of basil
- 1 ½ cups sour cream

Melt butter in a pan. Add zucchini and onion. Add water and bouillon cubes. Mix. In a medium bowl combine: milk, salt, pepper, basil, and sour cream. Blend both mixtures in blender. Reheat slowly on stove. Enjoy!

SALADS

Recipe: <u>24 Hour Salad</u>

- 1 head of lettuce, broken up
- ½ cup celery, chopped
- ½ cup green peppers, chopped
- 10 oz pkg frozen peas
- 1 red onion, sliced
- 2 tbs sugar
- 2 cups mayonnaise
- 2 cups grated cheese, your choice
- 8-9 slices of bacon, cooked and crumbled

Layer the lettuce, celery, pepper, peas, and onion, in order, into a 9"x13" inch pan. Sprinkle sugar on top. Spread mayonnaise like icing. Spread cheese all over. Put bacon over top. Cover with foil, leave overnight, and cut into squares to serve. Enjoy!

Serves 24

Recipe: <u>Texas Beet Salad</u>

- 1 small pkg lemon jello
- 1 cup boiling water
- 2 – 9 oz jars strained baby food beets
- ½ pt sour cream
- 1 tsp lemon juice
- 1 tsp grated onion
- dash of salt and pepper to taste

Dissolve gelatin in hot water and let cool a little. Blend in other ingredients. Pour into four individual salad molds or one large one. Serve on lettuce with a little mayonnaise or your favorite dressing. Enjoy!

Recipe: <u>Raspberry Applesauce Mold</u>

- 3 pkg red raspberry jello
- 2 cups boiling water
- 2 pkg frozen raspberries
- 2 cups applesauce
- ¾ cup chopped nuts
- 1 lg pkg cream cheese
- 4 tbs milk
- 4 tbs confectioners' sugar

Mix jello and water. Stir in frozen raspberries. When raspberries are melted, add applesauce and nuts. Pour into mold and refrigerate. Serve with sauce. Mix cream cheese, milk and confectioners' sugar in blender and refrigerate leftovers. Enjoy!

Recipe: <u>Maple Salad Dressing</u>

- 2 eggs, beaten
- juice of 1 lemon
- 1 tbs flour
- 1 tbs sugar
- dash of salt
- ½ cup maple syrup
- 1 tsp butter
- ½ tsp vanilla
- whipping cream or cool whip

Beat eggs; add lemon juice, flour, sugar, salt and maple syrup. Boil until thick. Add butter and vanilla. When cold, thin with equal parts of whipping cream or cool whip and serve over any fruit salad. Enjoy!

Recipe: <u>Tuna Salad</u>

- 1 pkg lime jello
- 3/4 cup boiling water
- ½ cup cold water
- 1 can white tuna, shredded
- 2 tbs lemon juice
- ½ tsp salt
- ½ cup mayonnaise
- ½ cup diced celery
- ½ cup chopped nuts
- 8 oz diced pimiento

Dissolve jello in boiling water, add cold water, and salt. Blend in mayonnaise and let stand until slightly set. Then blend in remaining ingredients. Refrigerate until ready to serve. Enjoy!

Recipe: <u>Cabbage Salad</u>

- 1 cabbage, shredded
- 1 green pepper, diced
- 1 small onion, minced
- 2 carrots, shredded
- 3 tbs sugar
- dash of salt

Chop veggies and mix. Then make dressing.

Dressing:

- 1/3 cup mayonnaise
- 1/3 cup sour cream
- 1 tbs cider vinegar
- 2 tsp sugar
- ¾ tsp salt
- 2 tsp Dijon mustard
- dash red pepper seasoning

Blend; pour over salad, toss and chill. Enjoy!

Recipe: <u>Pineapple Mold</u>

- 1 pkg lemon jello
- 1 pkg lime jello
- 2 cups hot water
- 1 - 20 oz can crushed pineapple

Keep refrigerated until syrupy. Then mix together,

- 1 lb carton small curd cottage cheese
- 1 cup salad dressing
- 1 can condensed milk, Eagle brand
- 1 chopped nut meats

Blend in jello, place in refrigerator for 2 hours or more. Enjoy!

Serves 12

Recipe: <u>Tomato Jellied Salad</u>

- 1 pkg lemon jello
- 1 can hunts tomato sauce
- 1 ½ cups boiling water
- 1 ½ tbs vinegar
- 1 tsp celery salt
- dash of pepper
- 2 to 3 dashes Worcestershire sauce
- dash onion salt

Dissolve jello in water, add other ingredients. When jellied, you may add, if desired, diced celery, green pepper, raw shredded carrots, and/or sliced olives. Enjoy!

Recipe: <u>Lime Gelatin Salad</u>

- 2 pkg lime jello
- 1 cup hot water
- 1 - 20 oz can crushed pineapple
- 1 pt sour cream

Dissolve gelatin in hot water. Add crushed pineapple and sour cream. Mix thoroughly. Place in mold to set. Serve with following dressing;

- 1 medium size container cool whip
- 3 tbs mayonnaise
- 1 tbs lemon juice
- 1 - 16 oz pkg thawed frozen strawberries

Fold mayonnaise and lemon juice into cool whip. Lastly, fold in strawberries. Enjoy!

Recipe: <u>Sour Cream Salad Dressing</u>

- 1 cup sour cream
- 2 cups tiny marshmallows
- 2-3 drops of red coloring

Combine sour cream and marshmallows. Let stand in refrigerator for 24 hrs. Whip to a smooth consistency, add coloring. Serve over molded fruit salad. Enjoy!

Serves 6-8

Recipe: <u>Peach Jello Salad</u>

- 1 large can sliced peaches, drained
- 2 pkg peach jello
- 2 ½ cups boiling water
- 1/2 cup drained peach juice
- ½ cup cold water

Mix jello and boiling water until dissolved. Add cold water and juice. When jello is very cold and begins to get syrupy, add the peach slices and pour into a mold.

- 1 pkg dream whip
- 1 pkg vanilla or lemon pudding mix

Beat one envelope dream whip according to directions on box. Mix one package of instant pudding mix using 1 cup liquid. Fold above together and completely cover peach salad mold. Enjoy!

Recipe: <u>Cream Mint Dressing</u>

- 4 tbs heavy cream
- 1 tbs vinegar
- ½ tsp salt
- 1/8 tsp paprika
- 1 tsp finely chopped mint

Beat cream until light but not too stiff. Add vinegar, salt, paprika and mint. Serve on lettuce or fresh fruit salad. Enjoy!

SEAFOOD

Recipe: <u>Clam Casserole</u>

- 1 can clams (about 8 oz)
- 6 tbs butter (3/4 stick)
- 2 tbs all purpose flour
- 1 egg
- 1 cup bread crumbs, soft and fine
- milk

Drain liquid from clams into 2-cup size measuring cup. Add enough milk to make 1 ½ cups. Melt half the butter in medium size saucepan. Stir in flour. Cook, stirring constantly until bubbly. Then, stir in the milk and oyster juice mixture. Continue cooking and stirring until mixture thickens and boils about one minute. Remove from heat and cool. Beat in egg and clams. Melt remaining butter in small frying pan. Stir in bread crumbs. Heat slowly, shaking pan constantly until crumbs are lightly toasted. Spoon half into greased 4-cup baking dish. Top with clam mixture. Sprinkle with rest of crumb mixture. Bake at 350F degrees for 25 minutes, or until heated through. Serve and enjoy!

Serves 4

Recipe: <u>My Favorite Shrimp Salad</u>

- 1 - 3 oz pkg lemon jello
- 1 cup boiling water
- ½ tsp salt
- 1 tbs onion juice
- ¼ cup mayonnaise
- 3 cups chopped celery
- 1 cup walnut meats, broken in small pieces
- ½ cup whipped cream, stiff
- 1/2 lb chopped pimento cheese
- 1 tsp green pepper, chopped fine
- 1 - 5 oz can small shrimp
- 3 hard boiled eggs, chopped

Prepare jello using only 1 cup water. Add salt and onion juice. Cool slightly. Add rest of ingredients and put into small ring mold or 9 5-oz individual ring molds. (Double recipe for large mold.) Refrigerate overnight. Serve and enjoy!

Serves 6

Recipe: <u>Gum Ju-Ju</u>

- 1 onion, fried in butter
- 1 cup boiled rice
- 1 can shrimp
- 1 can tomato soup
- ½ pt cream
- salt and pepper

Mix all ingredients, heat in double boiler and serve on crackers. Enjoy!

Serves 4

Recipe: <u>Tuna Scallop Royale</u>

- 2 avocados
- salt
- 1 can condensed mushroom soup
- 1 can tuna
- potato chips

Cut avocados in halves (lengthwise), remove seed and add salt. Combine undiluted soup with tuna and heat thoroughly in a pan. Place avocado halves in baking pan containing ¼" warm water. Fill generously with tuna mixture. Cover with crushed chips. Bake at 325F degrees for 10-15 minutes. Garnish with lemon wedges. Enjoy!

Serves 4

Recipe: <u>Scalloped Oysters</u>

- 1 ½ pt oysters
- 1 ½ pt liquor
- 3 tbs milk
- ¾ cup stale bread crumbs
- 1 ½ cups cracker crumbs
- ¾ cup melted butter
- ¼ cup sherry
- salt and pepper

Layer oysters and crumbs in casserole. Bake at 350F degrees for 30-40 minutes. Serve and enjoy!

Recipe: <u>Mothers Fish and Lobster Casserole</u>

- 1 ½ lb any white fish
- ½ lb scallops
- ½ lb lobster meat
- ½ lb shrimp
- ½ lb butter
- ½ bottle clam juice
- 1/3 cup milk
- 1 small pkg Ritz crackers, crumbled fine

Mix butter with crumbs. Divide into 3 parts. Cut up fish, scallops, shrimp and mix with cut up lobster meat. Place in casserole dish alternating layers with crumbs. Add clam juice and milk. Mix in a few drops of Tabasco sauce. Bake at 325F degrees for approximately 30 minutes or until tender. Enjoy!

Serves 6

Recipe: <u>Broiled Scrod A La Parker</u>

- 1 lb Scrod
- 1 tsp salt
- 1 tsp pepper
- ½ cup flour
- ½ cup olive oil
- ½ cup bread crumbs

Season scrod with salt and pepper, dredge with flour, dip in olive oil, then flavored bread crumbs. Broil 6 minutes on each side Serve with lemon and parsley. Enjoy!

Recipe: <u>Lobster Newburg</u>

- ¼ cup butter
- ½ tsp paprika
- 1/3 cup sherry
- 1 lb cooked lobster
- 2 tbs flour
- 2 egg yolks
- 2 cups cream

In double boiler; stir to melt butter. Add paprika and sherry. Stir. Add lobster. Cook for a minute or two. Sprinkle flour over and blend gently. Separately beat eggs and cream. Add to lobster mixture and fold in until well blended. Should be thick and smooth. Serve on toast or patty shells. Enjoy!

Recipe: <u>Seafood Au Gratin</u>

- 1 can cream of celery soup
- ¼ cup water
- 2 tbs white wine (optional)
- 2 cups cooked fish, crab, lobster, shrimp etc.
- ½ cup shredded mild cheese
- 1 tbs minced parsley

Mix. Put in greased 10"x6"x2" baking dish. Bake at 400F degrees for 20 minutes. Enjoy!

Serves 3-4

Recipe: <u>Tuna Divan</u>

- 1 bunch broccoli, cut up
- 1 - 12 ½ oz can tuna, drained and flaked
- ¼ cup real mayonnaise
- 1 tbs corn oil
- 1 tbs cornstarch
- 1 cup milk
- 1 cup sharp cheddar cheese, grated
- ¼ cup fine dry bread crumbs
- 1 tbs parsley flakes

In 1 cup boiling salted water, cook broccoli until tender-crisp. Drain and arrange in well greased 10"x6"x2" inch casserole. Top with flaked tuna. In a 2 quart sauce pan stir together mayonnaise, cornstarch and seasonings until smooth. Stir in milk gradually, and then blend in cheese. Bring to one minute boil, stirring constantly. Pour over tuna and broccoli. Combine crumbs, parsley and oil. Sprinkle over sauce. Bake in 350F degree oven until hot and bubbly. Enjoy!

Serves 4-5

Recipe: <u>Crabmeat Rim Tuna Ditty</u>

- ½ lb butter
- 1 cup sharp cheddar cheese, grated
- 1 can of undiluted tomato soup
- 1 can crab meat
- ½ pt cream
- 1 egg, beaten

Melt butter; add cheese, tomato soup, crabmeat, and cream. Cook slowly 20 minutes on low heat. Add egg. Stir in gently. Serve on buttered toast. Enjoy!

Recipe: <u>Quick and Easy Tuna Pies</u>

- 1 pkg (10 oz) frozen patty shells
- 2 cans (7 oz) tuna, drained and flaked
- 1 can or jar (4 oz) pimiento, drained and diced
- 4 hard cooked eggs, chopped
- 2 cans condensed golden mushroom soup
- ½ cup milk

Bake patty shells as directed. Cut off center top. Mix all other ingredients together in saucepan. Bring to boil and simmer for 5 minutes until well heated. Serve by mounding a tablespoon or two on each plate, top with a patty shell, spoon remaining mixture into shells and replace tops. Enjoy!

Serves 6

Recipe: <u>Shrimp Cinta</u>

- 1 cup lemon juice
- 1 cup olive oil
- 6 cloves garlic, crushed
- 2 tsp parsley
- 1 tsp red pepper (optional
- 24 large shrimp, shelled and deveined

Combine all ingredients, pour over shrimp and marinate overnight in refrigerator. Remove shrimp and broil until brown or about 5 minutes on each side. Enjoy!

Serves 4

Recipe: <u>Shrimp and Cheese Casserole</u>

- 1 lb prepared shrimp, or ¼ lb bag of frozen shrimp
- 6 slices of bread, crusts removed, broken in pieces
- ½ lb bag old English cheese, cut up
- ¼ cup margarine or butter, melted
- ½ tsp dry mustard
- 3 well beaten eggs
- 1 pt milk
- salt and pepper to taste
- shake of onion powder, if desired

Shake onion powder in greased casserole. Pour melted butter over this. Combine milk, eggs and other ingredients. Blend gently and pour over first ingredients in casserole. Let stand 3 hours. Bake 1 hour at 350F degrees. Enjoy!

Serves 4-5

Recipe: <u>Cheese Fondue</u>

Serves 6

- 1 cup scalded milk
- 1 cup soft bread crumbs
- ½ lb mild cheese, cut in small pieces
- 1 tbs butter
- 1 tsp salt
- 3 egg yolks, save egg whites

Mix milk, bread crumbs, cheese, butter and salt together. Add egg yolks. Beat egg whites, stir and fold in. Bake 20 minutes at 350F degrees. Enjoy!

Recipe: <u>Baked Fillets with Puffy Cheese Sauce</u>

- 2 lb frozen fillets
- ¼ cup mayonnaise
- 1 tbs chopped sweet pickle
- ¼ cup grated cheddar cheese
- 2 egg yolks, beaten
- 2 egg whites, beaten

Thaw frozen fish and cut into serving size pieces. Place in single layer in well greased baking pan. Combine mayonnaise, pickle, cheese and egg yolks. Fold in beaten egg whites. Cover fish with sauce. Bake at 350F degrees for 30 minutes. Fish should be flakey and sauce brown. Serve and enjoy!

Recipe: <u>Welsh Rarebit</u>

- 1 tbs butter
- 1 tsp cornstarch
- ½ tsp salt
- ½ tsp mustard
- 1 cup milk
- 2 eggs, well beaten
- 1 lb diced cheese

Cook in double boiler, add diced cheese last. Stir until melted. Enjoy!

CHICKEN

Recipe: <u>Chicken and Wild Rice Casserole</u>

- 1 pkg wild rice
- 1 - 8 oz can mushroom pieces
- 1 ½ cups chicken and mushroom broth
- 1 ½ cups light cream
- ¼ cup flour
- ¼ cup soft butter
- 1 ½ tsp salt
- ¼ tsp pepper
- 1 small onion, quartered
- 1 - 2 oz jar pimento
- 3 cups cubed chicken
- ½ cup slivered almonds
- parsley

Heat oven to 350F degrees. Butter 2 quart casserole dish. Prepare rice according to package directions. While rice cooks, drain mushrooms, reserve and add liquid to measure 1 ½ cups and pour into blender. Add all ingredients except chicken and almonds, cover and process on high. Cook mushrooms, chicken and sauce. Sprinkle with almonds. Bake 25-35 minutes. Enjoy!

Recipe: <u>Crispy Drumsticks</u>

- 24 chicken legs
- ½ cup flour
- 1 tsp salt
- ½ tsp paprika
- 1/8 tsp pepper
- 2 eggs, slightly beaten
- 3 tbs milk
- 3 ½ cups coarsely crushed rice krispies
- 1 envelope onion soup mix
- ½ cup grated parmesan cheese
- 6 tbs butter

Wash chicken and pat dry. Combine in paper bag, flour, salt, paprika and pepper. Shake a few chicken legs at a time until coated all over. Shake off excess flour. In a shallow dish, combine eggs and milk. In another dish combine rice cereal, soup mixture and cheese. Roll chicken legs in milk, then cereal and arrange on pans. Bake at 350F degrees for 45 minutes. Serve hot or cold. Enjoy!

Recipe: <u>Wood Chuck</u>

- 5 hard cooked eggs
- 1 small can pimentos, cut fine
- 1 small green pepper, cut fine
- ½ lb grated American cheese
- 1 can sliced mushrooms

(For cream sauce)

- ½ stick butter
- 2 cups milk
- 2 tbs flour

Make light cream sauce, add cheese and other ingredients. Cook until cheese melts and all ingredients blend. Serve on Chinese noodles. Enjoy!

Recipe: <u>Sunday Chicken</u>

- 2 tbs butter
- 2 tsp curry powder
- 1 apple, with skin, chopped
- 1 onion, chopped
- 6 skinned, boned, chicken breasts
- 1 can condensed cream of mushroom soup (add fresh mushrooms if you like)
- 1 cup light cream
- salt and pepper

Sauté apple, onion and curry in butter. Add to soup and cream.

Place chicken in one layer in lightly greased pan. Add seasonings. Pour sauce over chicken. Bake uncovered at 350F degrees for 1 ½ hours (less time with boneless, skinless breasts. Enjoy!

Recipe: <u>Quick and Easy Oven Fried Chicken</u>

- 2 ½ lb broiler - fryer chicken
- ½ cup flour
- ¼ cup bread crumbs
- 1 tsp salt
- 1 tsp paprika
- ¼ tsp pepper
- 3 tbs oil
- 3 tbs oleo

Rinse chicken. Mix crumbs, flour, salt, pepper and paprika in plastic bag. Meanwhile, heat oil and oleo in 425F degrees oven in 13"x9" baking pan. Shake chicken in bag of seasoned flour and place in baking pan. Bake uncovered 25-30 minutes at 425F degrees. Turn chicken. Cook uncovered for 20-30 minutes longer. Check after 20 minutes. Serve hot or cold. Enjoy!

Recipe: <u>Hawaiian Chicken</u>

* 2 ½ - 3 lb broiler - fryer, halved, quartered or pieces of chicken
* 1 tsp monosodium glutamate
* 1 can pineapple chunks
* 1 cup basic barbecue sauce ***
* ½ tsp salt
* ¼ tsp ginger
* 1 tsp soy sauce
* 2 tsp cornstarch
* 1 tbs cold water or syrup
* ½ medium green pepper, diced
* 1 can mandarin oranges, drained
* 6 maraschino cherries, halved

Sprinkle halves with monosodium glutamate. Place skin side down in shallow baking dish, set aside. Drain pineapple chunks, measure ½ cup syrup. Add syrup and bbq in sauce pan. Stir in salt, ginger and soy sauce. Blend cornstarch with cold water. Blend with sauce. Bring to boil, reduce heat and simmer for 5 minutes. Brush chicken with mixture. Bake chicken at 350F degrees for 1 hour. Brushing occasionally with sauce and turning over once every 30 minutes. Add pineapple chunks, green pepper, mandarin oranges and cherries to remaining sauce. Heat and pour over the last 5 minutes of baking time. Serve and enjoy!

Serves 5

Basic Barbeque Sauce

* ½ cup molasses
* 2 tbs mustard
* ½ cup vinegar
* 4 drops hot pepper sauce

Mix together and ready to serve. Enjoy!

Recipe: <u>Chicken and Rice</u>

White Sauce:

- 5 tbs sifted flour
- 1 tsp salt
- ¼ tsp onion salt
- ¼ cup melted butter
- 2 1/2 cups half and half cream

Main Dish:

- 1 1/3 cups minute rice
- 1 ½ cups chicken broth
- ¼ cup grated cheese
- 1 ½ box frozen asparagus or broccoli
- Turkey or Chicken slices
- ¼ cup American cheese

Make white sauce and set aside. Put rice in 2 quart flat pan. Pour broth over rice. Sprinkle cheese. Top with broccoli or asparagus. Cover with meat and sprinkle more cheese on top. Pour white sauce over and top with toasted almonds. Bake at 375F degrees for 20 minutes. Enjoy!

Serves 6

Recipe: <u>Chicken and Zucchini Casserole</u>

- 3 medium zucchini, about 1 lb, washed
- 2 ½ - 3 lb chicken pieces
- salt and pepper to taste
- 2/3 cup bottled bbq sauce
- 1 tsp dried oregano leaves
- 1 tbs lemon juice
- 1 tsp instant minced onion

Heat oven to 400F degrees. Slice unpeeled zucchini crosswise into slices about 1/4" inch thick. Arrange along bottom of shallow 3 qt baking dish. Sprinkle chicken with salt and pepper. Place chicken skin side up over zucchini. In a small bowl, combine remaining ingredients and pour over chicken. Bake uncovered for 30 minutes. Baste with sauce from bottom of dish and return to oven 30 minutes more. Enjoy!

Recipe: <u>Chicken Divan for Two</u>

- 1 cup cooked, cut up broccoli
- 1 cup cooked, cubed chicken (or tuna)
- 1 can cream of chicken soup
- ¼ cup mayonnaise
- ½ tsp curry powder
- 1 ½ tsp lemon juice
- paprika

Layer broccoli, then chicken in bottom of pan or casserole dish. Combine soup, mayonnaise, curry powder and lemon juice. Spread over chicken. Sprinkle with paprika. Bake 350F degrees for 35-40 minutes or until hot. Enjoy!

Serves 2

Recipe: <u>Babas Chicken and Rice Squares</u>

- 4 ½ cups chicken, cut into chunks
- 1 cup rice, cooked as directed on box (not instant rice)
- 2 large eggs
- ½ cup almonds, slivered
- ¼ cup pimentos, chopped
- 2 tbs butter
- ½ tsp paprika
- 1 ½ cups broth
- ½ cup milk
- 2 tbs parsley flakes
- 2 tsp onion flakes
- ½ tsp celery salt
- salt and pepper to taste

Sauce:

- 1 can mushroom soup
- ¼ cup chicken broth

Beat eggs in bowl, add remaining ingredients and blend. Put in greased 9"x13" inch pan. Bake 30-40 minutes at 350F degrees. Let stand 15 minutes before serving. Cut into squares and serve with sauce. Enjoy!

MEATS

Recipe: <u>Hawaiian Meat Balls</u>

- 1 ½ lb ground beef
- 2/3 cup cracker crumbs
- ½ cup chopped onion
- 2/3 cup evaporated milk
- 1 tsp seasoned salt
- 1/3 cup flour
- 3 tbs shortening

Combine first 5 ingredients, mix lightly but thoroughly. Shape meat mixture into 30 balls. Roll in flour. Brown meat balls in shortening. Drain excess fat. Meanwhile prepare Sweet and Sour sauce.

- 1 can pineapple chunks
- 2 tbs cornstarch
- ½ cup vinegar
- ½ cup brown sugar
- 2 tbs soy sauce
- 2 tbs lemon juice
- 1 cup coarsely chopped green pepper
- 1 tbs chopped pimiento

Drain pineapple chunks, reserve pineapples. Measure syrup. Add water to make 1 cup liquid. Blend together pineapple liquid and cornstarch until smooth. Stir in next 4 ingredients. Cook until thickened and clear. Add pineapple, green pepper and pimiento. Mix well. Cover and simmer over low heat for 15 minutes. Pour Sweet and Sour sauce over chicken. Serve with rice and orange-avocado salad. Enjoy!

Serves 6

Recipe: <u>Pepper Steak Beef Dish</u>

- 1 ½ lb inch thick steak
- ¼ cup salad oil
- 1 clove garlic, minced
- 3 small onions, sliced
- pinch of thyme
- ½ cup tomato puree
- 3 medium green peppers, cut into 1" inch strips
- ½ tsp sugar
- 1 tsp salt
- ½ tsp pepper
- 1 ½ cups cold water

Cut meat into inch strips. Brown in oil, stirring often for 20 minutes. Add onions and garlic during last minutes of browning. Add seasonings, tomato puree, and ½ cup water. Cover and simmer until meat is tender, about one hour. Stir occasionally and add water as evaporation occurs while cooking. Add peppers and cook 15 minutes longer. Serve with noodles and whipped potatoes. Enjoy!

Recipe: <u>Parmesan Meat Loaf</u>

- 1 lb ground beef
- 1 cup large curd cottage cheese
- ½ cup quick oats
- 1 egg
- ¼ cup catsup
- 2 tsp mustard
- 2 tbs chopped onion
- 1 tsp salt
- dash pepper
- 1/3 cup grated parmesan cheese

Thoroughly mix all ingredients, except parmesan cheese. Lightly pack mixture in 8"x4"x2" inch pan or small bread pan. Bake at 350F degrees in oven for 20 minutes. Sprinkle parmesan cheese on top. Bake 10 more minutes. Let it stand for 5 minutes before serving. Enjoy!

Recipe: <u>Beef Italiano'</u>

- 1 ½ lb blade steak
- 2 cans of tomato sauce
- 1 can mushrooms, drained
- 1 tsp oregano
- garlic salt to taste
- pepper to taste
- ½ lb provolone cheese

Place finely cubed beef on bottom of oblong baking dish. Place tomato sauce on top of beef; add mushrooms, garlic, salt, pepper and oregano. Space cheese evenly over top. Bake 1 hour at 350F degrees. Enjoy!

Serves 6

Recipe: <u>Frankfort Casserole</u>

- 1 pkg Birdseye mixed vegetables with onion sauce
- ¾ cup milk
- ½ lb franks
- 2 oz shredded cheese
- ½ cup bread crumbs

Combine veggies, mix with milk in saucepan, and follow directions on package. Stir in franks (cut up). Spoon ½ into an ungreased 6 cup baking dish. Mix crumbs and cheese. Sprinkle over mixture. Top with veggie mix and the remaining crumbs. Bake at 375F degrees for 30 minutes. Enjoy!

Working Mother's Dinner For Four in 20 minutes

- Chili Con Carne (see recipe below)
- Mashed Potatoes
- Relish Tray; Carrot And Celery Sticks, Radishes and Olives
- Hot Rolls
- Ice Cream

Recipe: Chili Con Carne

- 1 lb ground beef
- ½ cup onions, chopped
- 1 can tomato soup
- 1 can red kidney beans
- 2-3 tbs chili powder
- 1 tbs cumin powder

Shake salt on heavy frying pan. Cook ground beef until brown. Add chopped onions and cook until translucent. Add rest of ingredients. Stir slowly until heated through. Enjoy! (If making whole dinner as listed above continue reading.) Prepare relish tray while chili is cooking. Mix instant mashed potatoes using slightly less milk than called for. Serve chili on top of potatoes. Enjoy!

Recipe: Savory Liver

- ¼ cup chopped onion
- 2 tsp chopped parsley
- 2 tbs butter
- 2 tbs flour
- ¾ tsp salt
- dash pepper
- 3 tbs vinegar
- 2 ½ cups beef bouillon
- 1 ½ lb liver

Brown onions and parsley in butter. Stir in flour, salt, pepper and vinegar. Add bouillon stirring constantly. Cook until thickened. Place liver in gravy and cook covered for 15 minutes, turning once. Serve and enjoy!

Serves 4

Recipe: <u>Supper Ham and Eggs</u>

- 2 cups cubed ham
- 4-5 hard cooked eggs, sliced
- 1 can sliced mushrooms
- 1 can cream of celery soup
- ¼ cup milk
- 1 cup sharp cheese, shredded
- 6 drops Tabasco
- 1 ½ cups soft bread crumbs
- ½ stick margarine

Alternate layers of ham, sliced eggs and mushrooms, ending with ham. Combine soup and milk. Add cheese and Tabasco. Heat and pour over ham etc. Top with buttered crumbs. Bake uncovered at 375F degrees for 25 minutes. Serve with green peas and pineapple coleslaw. Enjoy!

Recipe: <u>Porcupines</u>

- ½ lb ground beef
- ¼ lb ground pork
- ¼ pound ground veal
- 1 small green pepper, diced
- 1 small onion, diced
- 1 egg
- ½ cup uncooked rice
- seasoning of choice to taste
- 1 can tomato soup
- 2 cans water

Mix the meats, veggies, egg, rice and seasonings together and form into small balls. Place into a waterless cooker and add soup and water. Simmer for 1 hour. Additionally, if preferred, add 1/8 tsp nutmeg, ¼ tsp salt and pepper to taste. Enjoy!

Recipe: <u>Bar-B-Que Sauce</u>

- 1/3 cup minced onion
- 3 tbs butter
- 1 cup catsup
- 1/3 cup vinegar or lemon juice
- 3 tbs brown sugar
- ½ cup water
- 2 tsp prepared mustard
- 2 tbs Worcestershire sauce
- Pinch pepper

Simmer 10 minutes. Serve hot. Enjoy!

Recipe: <u>Macaroni and Cheese</u>

- ½ lb macaroni, cooked and drained
- 1 tbs butter
- 1 egg, beaten
- 1 cup milk
- 1 tsp salt
- 1 tsp dry mustard
- 1 tbs hot water
- 3 cups grated cheese, sharp

Add butter to cooked, drained macaroni. Mix egg and milk. Mix salt and mustard with hot water and add milk to it. Add cheese, saving some to sprinkle on top. Mix milk and cheese mixture with macaroni in buttered casserole dish. Sprinkle with remaining cheese. Bake uncovered at 350F degrees for 45 minutes or until mixture is set up and the top is crusty. Enjoy!

Recipe: <u>No Crust Quiche</u>

- 3 eggs
- 1/3 cup bisquick
- ½ cup melted butter
- 1 ½ cups milk or a creamed soup
- ¼ tsp salt
- dash pepper
- 1 cup shredded Swiss cheese

optional:

- ½ cup bacon, fried and crumbled
- ham bits
- onion or mushroom bits

Beat eggs lightly; add bisquick, melted butter, milk or soup and seasonings. Pour into greased 9" inch pie pan. Sprinkle with shredded cheese and any of the optional ingredients. Bake uncovered for 45 minutes. at 350F degrees. Let stand 10 minutes before serving. Enjoy!

Serves 4-6

VEGETABLES

Recipe: <u>Zucchini Quick</u>

- 4 cups thin sliced zucchini
- 1 onion, chopped
- ½ cup oil
- 1 cup bisquick
- 4 eggs, beaten
- 1 tsp salt
- 2 tsp parsley
- ¼ tsp basil
- ½ cup parmesan cheese

Mix together by hand. Bake uncovered in 350F degree oven for 30 minutes in 9"x13" inch pan. Enjoy!

Serves 4-6

Recipe: <u>Squash Casserole</u>

- 2 lb yellow squash
- 1 medium onion, grated
- 1 large carrot, grated
- 1 carton sour cream – 8 oz
- 1 can cream of chicken soup
- ½ stick butter
- ½ pkg Pepperidge farm stuffing

Cook squash with salt and pepper to taste, until tender. Drain and mash. Mix sour cream and undiluted chicken soup. Add onion and carrot. Fold this into squash. Pour into buttered oblong baking dish. Add stuffing on top. Dot with butter. Bake at 350F degrees for 30 minutes. Enjoy!

Recipe: <u>Zucchini Pie</u>

- 4 cups zucchini, thinly sliced and unpeeled
- 1 cup chopped onion
- ½ cup butter
- 2 tbs parsley flakes
- ½ tsp salt
- ½ tsp black pepper
- ¼ tsp garlic powder
- ¼ tsp basil
- ¼ tsp oregano
- 2 eggs
- 2 cups mozzarella or muenster cheese, shredded
- 8 oz can crescent rolls
- 2 tsp mustard

Cook together zucchini and onion in butter 10 minutes or until tender. Stir in next 6 ingredients. In separate bowl, beat the 2 eggs and add shredded cheese. Stir into veggie mixture. Place crescent rolls on side and bottom of ungreased 8" inch pie plate. Spread mustard on bottom crust. Pour vegetable mixture into pie pan. Bake at 375F degrees for 18-20 minutes. Let stand for 10 minutes before serving. Enjoy!

Recipe: <u>Belgium Potatoes</u>

- 4-5 potatoes
- 1 stick butter
- 1 tbs lemon juice
- 1/8 tsp paprika
- pepper to taste
- 1 tsp salt

Slice potatoes thin and soak in ice water for 1 to 2 hours to remove starch. Dry potatoes very well in paper towels and place in greased casserole in layers. Pour ½ butter mixture over potatoes. Place in 400F degree oven for ½ hour. Take out and pour rest of butter over, mix thoroughly. If you would like it tart, add a little more lemon. Return to oven and cook until done. Last few minutes dust paprika over it. Enjoy!

Recipe: <u>Corn Soufflé</u>

- 2 tbs butter, melted
- 2 tbs flour
- 1 cup scalded milk
- 1 can corn
- salt and pepper to taste
- celery salt, optional
- 2 egg yolks, well beaten
- 2 egg whites

Melt the butter, add flour and blend. Pour in milk gradually while stirring. Bring to boiling point and add corn. Season with salt and pepper. Add egg yolks. Separately beat egg whites until stiff and fold into mixture. Bake in 350F degree oven until firm. Enjoy!

Recipe: <u>Eggplant Casserole</u>

- ½ can mushroom soup
- ½ cup mayonnaise
- 1 egg
- 1 large eggplant, cubed, cooked in salt water, and dried
- 1 tbs grated onion
- ¾ cup Ritz cracker crumbs
- 1/3 stick butter
- 1 cup shredded sharp cheese

Mix soup, mayonnaise, beaten egg, onion and cheese with eggplant. Put in casserole dish. Cover with crumbs, dot with butter. Bake at 350F degrees for 15-20 minutes. Enjoy!

Recipe: <u>Baked Celery</u>

- ½ lb sliced mushrooms
- ½ tsp salt
- ¼ tsp pepper
- 2 tbs butter
- 2 tbs flour
- ½ cup milk
- ½ cup grated sharp cheese
- 3 cups celery, 1" inch pieces, cooked

Sauté mushrooms in butter for 5 minutes. Sprinkle with flour, salt and pepper and blend. Add milk and cook until thick and smooth. Place celery in a shallow baking dish and cover with mushrooms. Sprinkle with cheese. Bake in 350F degree oven for 15 minutes. Enjoy!

Serves 6

Recipe: <u>Baked Scalloped Orange Beets</u>

- 5 tbs dry bread crumbs, divided
- 3 tbs sugar
- 1 can sliced beets, drained
- ½ cup orange juice
- 1 tsp vinegar
- 1 tbs butter, melted

Mix 3 tbs breadcrumbs with sugar. In greased 1 qt baking dish alternate layers of beets and crumb mixture. Pour orange juice and vinegar over all. Cover and bake in preheated 350F degree oven 20 minutes or until bubbling. Mix remaining 2 tbs crumbs with butter. Sprinkle over beets. Return to oven. Bake uncovered, 7 minutes or until crumbs are lightly browned. Enjoy!

Serves 4

Recipe: <u>Bourbon Baked Beans</u>

- 4 cans baked beans
- 2 medium size oranges, sliced
- 1 cup seedless raisins
- 1 cup molasses
- ¼ tsp ground ginger
- ½ cup bourbon
- 1 medium lemon, sliced

Combine beans, oranges, lemon, raisins, molasses and ginger in a shallow 3 qt baking dish. Mix well. Gradually add bourbon and mix to blend. Bake in oven at 300F degrees for 40 minutes or until heated through and flavors have blended. Enjoy!

Serves 8

Recipe: <u>Scalloped Onions with Cheese</u>

- 6 large white onions
- milk, enough to cover onions
- 4 slices buttered toast
- 1 cup grated cheddar cheese
- 1 egg
- 1 cup milk
- ½ tsp salt
- 1/8 tsp paprika

Peel and slice onions into rings. Poach in milk, drain well. Place toast in a buttered baking dish. Arrange onions on top and sprinkle on cheese. Beat together egg, milk, salt and paprika: pour over onions. Dot with butter. Bake 40 minutes at 350F degrees. Serve with crisp bacon and parsley on top. Enjoy!

Recipe: <u>Tomato Marmalade</u>

- 4 lb ripe tomatoes
- 5 cups sugar
- 1 lemon

Scald and peel tomatoes. Leave whole. Add sugar and let stand overnight. Add thinly sliced lemon and cook until mixture is clear and thick. Makes approximately 8 jellies. Enjoy!

Recipe: <u>Tomato Pie</u>

- 2 cups bisquick mix
- 2/3 cup milk
- tomatoes, sliced thin, and peeled
- chopped chives
- fresh basil
- 1 cup sharp grated cheese
- 1 cup mayonnaise
- chopped onion

Mix bisquick and milk. Press into 10 or 12 inch pie plate, lightly greased. Layer tomatoes and between layers, sprinkle remaining ingredients plus salt and pepper. Mix cheese and mayonnaise and spread over top. Bake 30 minutes at 400F degrees. Can be made and reheated or frozen. Enjoy!

BREADS

Recipe: <u>Swedish Coffee Cake</u>

- 1 ½ cups milk
- ¾ cup sugar
- ½ cup shortening
- ¼ tsp salt
- 6 cups flour, sifted and divided in half
- 1 yeast cake dissolved in
- ¼ cup warm water
- 2 eggs
- 8-10 cardamon seeds***

Bring milk to boiling point and pour over sugar, shortening and salt. Let stand until warm. Add yeast and 3 cups flour. Let rise until double in size. Then add eggs, cardamom seeds and more flour. Knead and let rise again. Punch down and divide dough into six sections. Roll each section out. Raisins may be placed in each section if desired. Braid dough together using three sections for each braid. Let rise. Bake at 350F degrees for 25-30 minutes. Check toward end of baking time because it may take less time. Enjoy!

***cardamom seeds should be opened and the small seeds inside crushed to a powder consistency. (A pestel and mortar are necessary.)

Recipe: <u>Bran Muffins</u>

- 1 ½ cups sifted flour
- 1 tsp baking soda
- ¼ tsp salt

After sifting generously;

- ½ cup bran
- 1 beaten egg
- 1 tbs fat
- 2 tbs molasses or brown sugar
- 1 cup sour milk

Mix together until combined. Bake at 350F degrees for 15-20 minutes until golden brown. Enjoy!

Makes 12 muffins

Recipe: <u>Nut Bread</u>

- 2 ½ cups graham flour
- 1 cup white flour
- ¾ cup sugar
- ¼ cup molasses
- 1 tbs lard
- 1 ½ cups sour milk
- 1 tsp baking soda
- 1 tsp salt
- 1 cup chopped nuts

Mix together. Bake 1 hour in oven at 325F degrees. Enjoy!

Recipe: <u>Ft. Atkinson Gingerbread</u>

- 2 tbs sugar
- ½ cup butter
- 2 heaping cups flour
- 1 tsp ginger
- 1 cup molasses
- 1 egg yolk, beaten
- 1 cup boiling water
- 1 tsp baking soda
- 1 egg white, beaten

Cream together sugar and butter. Rub flour and ginger into butter and sugar until fine. Add molasses. Add yolk. Add water and baking soda. Add egg white and fold in. Bake at 375F degrees 10-15 minutes or until golden brown. Enjoy!

Recipe: <u>Special Corn Muffins</u>

- ½ cup regular yellow corn meal
- ½ cup regular flour
- 3 tsp baking powder
- 1 tbs sugar
- ½ tsp salt
- ¾ cup milk
- 1 egg, well beaten
- 1 tbs vegetable or corn oil
- 1 tbs chopped green and red pepper
- 1 tsp onion, chopped fine
- ½ cup grated sharp cheddar

Sift together corn meal, flour, baking powder, sugar and salt. Add milk and egg. Blend together with oil, peppers, onion and cheese. Pour into buttered muffin tins or corn-stick pan. Bake at 375F degrees for 25 minutes. These are colorful and can be easily frozen and stored. To reheat just place in aluminum foil in warm oven. Enjoy!

Makes 1 dozen

Recipe: <u>Blueberry Muffins</u>

- ¾ cup sugar
- 1 tbs butter
- ¼ tsp salt
- 1 egg
- ½ cup milk
- 1 ½ cups flour
- 1 tsp cream of tartar
- ½ tsp baking soda
- large cup blueberries

Mix sugar and butter. Add egg. Sift dry ingredients and add with milk. Stir lightly (a little dry flour showing won't hurt). Add blueberries. Fill cupcake pans ¾ full. Bake at 375F degrees about 15 to 20 minutes or until firm on top. Enjoy!

Recipe: <u>Danish Pastry</u>

Filling:

- ¼ cup sugar
- 2 rounded tsp cinnamon
- 1 cup chopped walnuts

Batter:

- ½ lb butter
- 2 cups flour, unsifted
- 1 egg yolk
- 1 cup sour cream

Mix filling separately and put aside. Cut in butter, add flour, beat in egg yolks and then add the sour cream. Batter should be very sticky. Shape dough into a ball, cover with flour. Wrap in waxed paper and put in refrigerator for at least an hour and a half (or a few days). After dough is chilled, remove and divide in half. Take each half and roll into a circle about 10" inches each. Fill the circles with filling and cut into 16 wedges each. Roll wedges from wide edge to narrow and bake rolled up. Bake in oven at 350F degrees in greased pan for 25-30 minutes until brown. Remove from pan immediately onto rack. Enjoy!

Makes 32 pieces

Recipe: <u>Quick Oatmeal Bread</u>

- 1 ½ cups boiling water
- ¾ cup rolled oats
- ¼ cup molasses
- 1 ½ tsp salt
- 3 tbs butter
- ¼ cup warm water (105F-115F)
- 1 pkg active dry yeast
- 3-4 cups sifted all purpose flour
- 1 tsp butter, for top

In medium bowl, pour boiling water over oats. Add molasses, salt and butter, stirring to mix well, then cool. In large bowl dissolve yeast in the water. Stir in oatmeal mixture. Gradually add 2 cups flour, at medium speed, beat 2 minutes. Mix in rest of flour by hand until well blended. Don't knead, it's batter bread. Cover top of bowl with towel or plastic wrap, let rise in warm place, free from drafts for 30 minutes. Grease a 9"x5"x3" inch pan with white shortening. With wooden spoon, stir batter 25 times and place pan to rise until ½ inch from top. Bake in preheated 425F degree oven 30 to 40 minutes. Butter top of bread, serve and enjoy!

Recipe: <u>German Pancakes</u>

- 6 tbs butter
- 6 eggs
- 1 cup milk
- 1 cup flour
- 1 tsp salt

In a 9"x12" or 9"x13" pan, put in butter. Melt over low heat. In blender or large bowl, add eggs, milk, flour and salt. Mix thoroughly. Pour batter into hot melted butter. Do not stir. Put in oven immediately. Bake 15 to 20 minutes at 425F degrees. Butter in oven must be hot when you put batter into it. Half recipe use 9 inch square pan. For 1/3 recipe use 8 inch square pan. Enjoy!

Recipe: <u>Sawyer Brown Bread</u>

- 1 cup flour, sifted
- 1 tsp baking soda, sifted
- ¼ cup sugar
- ½ cup cornmeal
- ½ tsp salt
- 1 tbs melted shortening
- 3 tbs molasses
- 1 cup milk
- 1 cup raisins

Mix all together with fork and pour into greased coffee can. Steam 2 or 3 hours until firm. Enjoy!

PUDDINGS

Recipe: <u>Brown Pudding</u>

- 1 qt milk
- 2 eggs
- 4 tbs cornstarch
- pinch of salt
- ¾ cup sugar
- 1 tsp vanilla
- 1 square chocolate

Scald milk. Meantime separate eggs, mix yolks, salt, sugar, cornstarch and a little cold milk. Add to hot milk. Stir until thick. Add vanilla. Beat egg whites and add sugar. Add melted chocolate and beat hard. Serve on top of pudding.

Serves 8-10

Recipe: <u>Steamed Blueberry Pudding</u>

- ½ cup sugar
- 1/3 cup butter
- 2 cups flour
- 2/3 cup sour milk
- 1 tsp baking soda
- 1/8 tsp salt
- 1 tbs molasses
- 1 egg
- 2 cups blueberries

Mix sugar, butter and egg together. Add rest of ingredients and stir until moist. Steam in greased pan 2 to 2 ½ hours until firm. Serve warm with whipped cream. Enjoy!

Recipe: <u>Buttercrunch Pudding</u>

- Box vanilla wafers
- ½ cup chopped walnuts
- ½ cup butter
- 1 cup confectioners' sugar
- 3 eggs yolks, save egg whites
- 1 ½ squares chocolate, melted

Crush wafers and mix together with walnuts. Cream butter and sugar. Add egg yolks. Beat with fork. Add chocolate. Beat egg whites until fluffy then add to chocolate mixture. Take ½ crumb mixture and put in buttered pan. Spread chocolate mixture on, then the rest of the cookie mix. Chill overnight. Delicious with dollop of vanilla ice cream or whipped cream. Enjoy!

Recipe: <u>Fruit Compote</u>

- 1 - 12 oz can frozen orange juice concentrate
- 1 - 12 oz can frozen pink lemonade
- 2 boxes frozen fruit cocktail
- 1 can crushed pineapple and juice
- 2 bananas, sliced
- 14 oz 7-Up soda pop
- frozen peaches, optional
- Royal Anne cherries, optional
- cinnamon and nutmeg to taste
- raisins or chopped apples, optional

Freeze in individual cups (5 oz). Remove 45 minutes before serving. Should still be a little bit frozen when served. Do not add water to orange juice or lemonade, but keep juice from cocktail. Enjoy!

Serves 20 to 24

Mix together first three ingredients. Stir in bread crumbs, cinnamon and nutmeg. Add fruit if desired. Dot with butter. Bake at 350F degrees about 1 hour in 2 quart casserole. Enjoy!

Recipe: <u>Bread Pudding</u>

- 3 eggs
- 3 cups milk
- 4 ½ tbs sugar
- 1 ½ tbs butter
- 3 slices bread, crumbled

Recipe: <u>Slump and Grunt</u>

- ½ cup water
- 1 qt blueberries
- 1 cup sugar
- 2 tbs butter
- 1 cup flour
- 2 tsp baking powder
- ½ tsp salt
- ¼ cup sugar
- ½ milk

There are two ways to cook this but ingredients remain the same.

1. **Slump:** in a deep skillet or wide bottom saucepan, stir water, berries and sugar. Bring to boiling point. Mix remainder of ingredients to a stiff batter. Spoon this over the berries as dumplings. Cover tightly and simmer for 12 minutes. Do not remove cover during this cooking time. Enjoy!

2. **Grunt:** preheat oven to 400F degrees. Grease deep baking dish or casserole and put water, cup of sugar and berries into this and put this into oven while mixing the topping dough. Blend butter into the flour. Add the rest of the ingredients. Spoon this over the hot berries and for 20 minutes. Enjoy!

Recipe: <u>Grandma's Plum Pudding</u>

- 1 small loaf white bread, sliced and buttered
- 1 qt milk
- ½ cup sugar
- ½ cup molasses
- 3 eggs
- 2 cups raisins
- 1 cup currants
- ½ cup candied fruits
- 1 tsp baking soda
- ½ tsp salt

Soak bread in milk until soft and mushy. Add remaining ingredients and mix. Just before cooking, add baking soda and salt. Bake 5 hours in greased pot, set in pan of water, in slow (250F degrees) oven. Enjoy!

Recipe: <u>Grape Nut Pudding</u>

- 3 eggs
- 1 cup sugar
- 1 cup grape nuts
- ½ tsp salt
- 1 qt milk
- 1 tsp vanilla
- 2 tbs melted butter

Mix together well. Let stand 10 minutes. Stir and bake in 350F degree oven for one hour. Enjoy!

Recipe: <u>Plum Pudding</u>

- 21 common crackers, ground
- 5 eggs, beaten
- 3 qts milk
- 1 tbs melted butter
- ½ tsp cloves
- ½ tsp nutmeg
- 1 tsp cinnamon
- 1 lb seedless raisins
- 5 oz candied mixed fruit
- 5 candied citron
- 5 oz candied orange peel
- 5 oz candied lemon peel
- 1 cup sugar
- ½ cup dark molasses
- 1 tsp salt
- 1 glass grape jelly
- 1 jigger of Brandy

Cook slowly for 5 hours or overnight in slow oven (225F-250F degrees) stirring every 20 minutes for 2 hours. Enjoy!

PIES

Recipe: <u>Pecan Pie</u>

- 3 eggs
- 1 cup light corn syrup
- 1/8 tsp salt
- 1 tsp vanilla
- 1 cup light brown sugar, packed
- 2 tbs butter
- 1 cup pecan halves
- 1 unbaked pie shell (9 inch size)

Preheat oven to 400F degrees. In a medium bowl beat eggs slightly. Add corn syrup, salt, vanilla, brown sugar and butter. Mix well. Stir in nuts and pour into unbaked pie shell. Bake for 15 minutes, reduce heat to 350F degrees and bake an additional 30 to 35 minutes, or until outer edge of filling seem set. Let cool completely on wire rack. Enjoy!

Recipe: <u>Rhubarb Pie</u>

- 3 cups rhubarb, cut into ½ inch pieces
- 1 cup sugar
- 2 tbs butter
- 2 tbs flour
- 1 egg (or two if small or medium)
- 1/8 tsp salt
- 1 tsp lemon juice or vinegar
- pie crust, top and bottom

Place above ingredients in an unbaked pie crust and cover with top crust. Bake at 425F degrees for 20 minutes, then at 375F degrees for 10 minutes. Enjoy!

Recipe: <u>Ritz Cracker Pie</u>

- 3 egg whites
- ½ tsp cream of tartar
- 1 cup sugar
- 12 Ritz crackers
- ½ cup chopped nuts

Beat egg whites until stiff. Add cream of tartar and sugar. Beat until you have stiff peaks and smooth. Remove from beaters. Fold in crackers and chopped nuts. Gently put into 9" pie plate, pushing meringue to sides of pan forming a cavity in the center. Bake at 325F degrees for 25 to 30 minutes, and then turn oven off and let pie cool in oven. When cool, fill center cavity with whipped cream. Enjoy!

Recipe: <u>Crumbly Top Apple Pie</u>

- 1 unbaked 9" pie shell
- 4 cups apple slices, pared and cut thin
- ¼ cup sugar
- ¾ tsp cinnamon
- ¼ tsp nutmeg
- 1/8 tsp salt
- ¾ cup brown sugar
- ¾ cup all purpose flour
- 1/3 cup butter

Mix together sugar, spices and salt with apples. Arrange apples into pie pan. Blend brown sugar, flour and butter. Mix with pastry blender until crumbly. Sprinkle over apples. Bake at 400F degrees for 30-35 minutes. Enjoy!

Recipe: <u>No Crust Squash Pie</u>

- 1 ½ cups milk
- ½ tsp salt
- 3 eggs
- ¼ cup vegetable oil or butter, melted
- 1/3 cup dark brown sugar
- 1 ¼ cups squash, cooked and mashed
- 1 tsp cinnamon
- ½ tsp ginger
- 1/8 tsp allspice
- ¼ tsp nutmeg or pumpkin pie spice
- ½ cup bisquick
- 1/3 cup granulated sugar

Put everything in a bowl and mix on high speed for 2-3 minutes. Pour into 9" or 10" inch greased pie pan. Let stand for 5 minutes, then bake at 350F degrees for 45 minutes or until knife is inserted in center comes out clean. Cool and serve. Enjoy!

Serves 6-8

CAKES

CAKES

Recipe: <u>Can't Wait Apple Cake</u>

- 4 cups apples, diced
- ½ cup cooking oil
- 1 ¼ cups sugar
- 2 eggs, well beaten
- 2 cups flour
- 1 ½ tsp baking soda
- ½ tsp salt
- ¾ tsp cinnamon
- 1 tsp vanilla
- 1 cup chopped walnuts

Combine apples, oil and sugar. Add beaten egg. Sift flour, soda, salt and cinnamon, and add to batter. Stir in vanilla and nuts. Bake in greased 9"x13" pan at 350F degrees until done. Enjoy!

Recipe: <u>Campbell's Tomato Soup Cake</u>

- 1 cup sugar
- ½ cup butter
- 1 can tomato soup
- 1 tsp soda
- 2 cups flour
- ½ tsp salt
- 2 tsp baking powder
- 1 tsp cinnamon
- ½ tsp cloves
- ½ tsp nutmeg
- 1 cup raisins
- 1 cup nuts (if desired)

For Frosting:

- 1 cup confectioners' sugar
- ¼ lb cream cheese
- 1 tsp vanilla

Cream together sugar and butter. In a bowl combine soup with baking soda. Add butter and sugar mixture with flour, salt, baking powder, spices, raisins and nuts. Mix together. Bake 1 hour in 350F degree oven. For frosting mix together until creamy and spread over cake. Enjoy!

Recipe: <u>Egg-less Milk-less Butter-less cake</u>

- 2 cups sugar
- 2 cups water
- 2 tbs lard
- 2 tsp cinnamon
- ½ tsp salt
- 1 pkg seedless raisins
- 3 cups flour
- 1 heaping tsp baking soda

Boil together sugar, water, lard, cinnamon, salt and seedless raisins. Add flour and baking soda. Mix well. Put into two well greased loaf pans and bake in 350F degree oven about one hour. Enjoy!

Recipe: <u>Pound Cake</u>

- 3 cups sugar
- 3 cups flour
- 3 sticks butter
- 5 eggs
- 1 tsp salt
- 1 tbs vanilla
- 1 cup evaporated milk

Cream sugar and butter. Add eggs, salt and vanilla. Add flour and mix together alternating with milk. Pour into floured and greased angel food cake pan. Bake in 350F degree oven for 1 hour and 45 minutes to 2 hours. Enjoy!

Recipe: <u>Sponge Cake</u>

- 3 eggs
- ¾ cup sugar
- 3 tbs water
- ½ tsp lemon extract
- ½ cup cake flour
- 3 tsp baking powder

Separate eggs. Beat yolks light and add sugar, water, lemon extract and flour. Beat whites a little, then add baking powder and beat until stiff. Fold in. Bake in ungreased pan in 350F degree oven for 25 minutes. Enjoy!

Recipe: <u>Easy Coffee Cake</u>

- 1 lb light brown sugar
- 2 eggs, beaten
- 1 cup strong coffee
- 1 cup Crisco oil
- 1 tsp vanilla
- 3 cups flour
- 1 tsp baking soda
- 1 tsp salt
- 1 cup chocolate bits
- 1 cup walnuts, chopped

In a bowl, sift flour, soda and salt. Add brown sugar. Mix coffee to beaten eggs and add this mixture to dry ingredients. Then add vanilla and vegetable oil. Grease large pan and spread batter. Top with chocolate bits and walnuts. Bake at 375F degree for 25 to 30 minutes. Enjoy!

Serves 12

Separate eggs. Beat yolks with cold water, and add sugar gradually. Add boiling water, and then fold in flour with baking powder and salt. Beat egg whites stiff and add cream of tartar. Pour batter into egg whites, mixing thoroughly by stirring. Bake 1 hour in 350F degree oven in a greased and floured tube pan. No frosting necessary. Sprinkle top with confectioners' sugar. Good with ice cream or fruit. Enjoy!

Recipe: <u>Sunshine Cake</u>

- 4 eggs
- 1 ½ cups sugar
- 1 tbs cold water
- 2/3 cup boiling water
- 1 ½ cups sifted flour
- 1 tsp baking powder
- 1 tsp cream of tartar
- ½ tsp salt
- 1 tsp vanilla

COOKIES

Recipe: <u>Irish Lace Cookies</u>

- ¾ cup firmly packed light brown sugar
- ½ cup butter, room temp
- 2 tbs flour
- 2 tbs milk
- 1 tsp vanilla
- 1 ¼ cups old fashioned rolled oats

Cream sugar and butter. Beat in flour, milk and vanilla. Stir in rolled oats. Drop mixture by teaspoons about 2" apart on a greased cookie sheet. Bake 10 minutes at 350F degrees. Remove from oven and let stand on cookie sheet for only one minute, then remove. Enjoy!

Recipe: <u>Apple Macaroon</u>

- 5 or 6 medium sized apples
- 1 cup sugar
- 1 cup flour
- 1 tsp baking powder
- 1 tsp salt
- ½ tsp cinnamon
- 1 egg

Pare, quarter and slice apples. Place in oblong baking dish and sprinkle with some sugar and cinnamon. Mix flour, sugar, salt and baking powder. Break eggs into dry ingredients and with fork mix together thoroughly until crumbly. Spread over apples and sprinkle rest of cinnamon over. Bake at 350F degrees for about 45 minutes, uncovered. Delicious served hot or cold and with ice cream. Enjoy!

Serves 6

Recipe: <u>Crispy Date Square</u>

Crust:

- 1 cup flour
- ½ cup brown sugar, packed
- ½ cup butter, softened

Combine until crumbly. Press into ungreased 9" square pan. Bake at 375F degrees for 10-12 minutes.

Filling:

- 1 cup chopped dates
- ½ cup sugar
- ½ cup butter
- 1 egg, beaten well
- 2 cups rice krispies
- 1 cup chopped nuts
- 1 tsp vanilla

Frosting:

- 2 cups powdered sugar
- 2-3 tsp milk
- ½ tsp vanilla
- 3 oz cream cheese

Combine dates, sugar and butter. Cook over medium heat until mixture boils, stirring constantly. Blend ¼ cup of mixture into beaten egg and return to saucepan. Cook until mixture just bubbles- stirring constantly. Remove from heat and stir in cereal, nuts and vanilla. Spread over baked crust and cool. Cream topping mixture and spread over filling. Cut into squares. Enjoy!

Makes approximately 24 squares

Recipe: <u>Minced Diamonds</u>

- 1 ½ cups flour
- 1 cup brown sugar
- ½ tsp salt
- ½ cup shortening
- 1 ¾ cups quick Quaker oats
- 2 cups mincemeat

Combine flour, brown sugar and salt. Cut in shortening with pastry blender. Mix in oats. Place half of mixture in bottom of 8"x8"x2" pan and press down. Spread with mincemeat, sprinkle remaining mixture over top. Bake in moderate oven (350F degrees) for 30 minutes. Cut into diamonds. Enjoy!

Makes 16

Recipe: <u>Arabian Macaroons</u>

- 1 1/3 cups flaked coconut
- ½ cup finely cut dates or figs
- ½ cup chopped walnuts
- ½ cup sugar
- 1/8 tsp salt
- 1 egg, well beaten
- ½ tsp vanilla

Combine coconut, dates, walnuts, sugar, and salt. Mix well. Blend in egg and vanilla. Drop from teaspoon onto cookie sheet. Bake at 350F degrees for 15 minutes or until golden brown. Remove at once from cookie sheet. Enjoy!

Recipe: <u>Butterscotch Bars</u>

- ½ cup butter
- 2 cups brown sugar
- 2 eggs
- 1 tsp vanilla
- 2 cups sifted flour
- 2 tsp baking powder
- ¼ tsp salt
- 1 cup shredded coconut
- 1 cup chopped walnuts.

In a 2 quart pan, melt butter. Remove from heat and stir in brown sugar. Add eggs one at a time beating well after each. Add vanilla. Sift together dry ingredients. Add with coconut and nuts to brown sugar mixture, stirring thoroughly. Spread in greased pan. Bake at 350F degrees about 25 minutes. Cut in bars while warm. Remove from pan when almost cool. Enjoy!

Makes 3 dozen

Recipe: <u>Chocolate Squares</u>

- 1 stick butter
- ½ cup salad oil
- 4 tbs cocoa
- 1 cup water
- 2 cups sugar
- 2 eggs
- ½ cup buttermilk
- 2 cups flour
- 1 tsp baking soda
- 1 tsp vanilla

Frosting:

- 1 stick oleo
- 4 tbs cocoa
- ½ cup buttermilk
- 1 lb confectioners' sugar
- ½ tsp salt
- 1 tsp vanilla
- 1 cup nuts

Heat butter, oil, cocoa and water in saucepan, over medium heat. Stir until mixed. Remove from heat, add sugar and milk. Make sure batter is slightly cooled before adding eggs. Add remaining ingredients. Mix thoroughly. Pour into greased and floured jelly roll pan. Bake at 400F degrees for 20 minutes. For frosting: boil oleo, cocoa, buttermilk. Add confectioners' sugar, vanilla, and nuts. Mix and pour over cake as soon as it comes out of the oven. Enjoy!

Recipe: <u>Monkey Cookies</u>

- 1 egg
- 1 cup sugar
- butter size of egg
- ½ cup sour milk
- ½ tsp baking soda
- 2 cups flour
- nutmeg
- salt to taste

Mix together, drop on buttered tin. Stick 3 raisins on top of each. Bake in 350F degree oven until golden brown. Enjoy!

Recipe: <u>Fruit Cake Cookies</u>

- ½ lb Citron
- ½ lb red candied cherries
- ½ lb green cherries
- ½ lb pineapple
- 1 lb raisins
- 1 cup Bourbon
- 1 lb chopped pecans
- 2 ½ cups flour
- 1 cup brown sugar
- 1 cup white sugar
- 3 eggs
- ½ cup butter
- 1 tsp salt
- 1 tsp baking soda

Sift salt and baking soda with flour. Combine butter, sugar and eggs. Add fruits (dusted with flour) and nuts. Bake at 325F degrees until golden. Do not brown. Enjoy!

Recipe: <u>Crispettes</u>

- 2 eggs
- 1 cup sugar
- 1 cup brown sugar
- 4 tbs sifted flour
- Pinch of salt
- 1 tsp vanilla
- 1 cup English walnuts, chopped fine

Beat eggs, stir in sugar, mixed with flour. Then salt and vanilla. Beat thoroughly and add walnuts. Drop dough by the teaspoon into buttered pans, allowing 3 inches to spread. Bake at 325F degrees for 8-10 minutes or until golden brown. Make sure not to burn! Delicious for afternoon tea. Enjoy!

Recipe: <u>Blueberry Crisp</u>

- 4 cups fresh blueberries
- 1 tsp grated lemon rind
- 1 cup quick rolled oats, uncooked
- 1 tsp ground cinnamon
- ½ cup flour
- ¼ cup brown sugar, firmly packed
- ½ cup butter, softened
- vanilla ice cream

Arrange blueberries in 10" baking dish. Sprinkle with lemon rind. In a bowl combine oats, cinnamon, flour and brown sugar. Cut in butter until evenly mixed and crumbly. Sprinkle over berries. Bake in preheated oven at 350F degrees for 25-30 minutes. Serve warm with ice cream. Enjoy!

Serves 6

Recipe: <u>Apple Crisp</u>

- 6-8 apples, sliced
- ¼ cup water
- ¾ cup CYO sugar
- ½ cup flour
- 1 tsp cinnamon
- 6 tbs butter
- ½ tsp salt

Peel and slice apples thin into a 2 qt baking dish. Add water. Combine sugar, flour, cinnamon and salt. Blend in the butter until crumbly in consistency. Pour over apples. Bake uncovered in 350F degree oven for about 1 hour. Enjoy!

Serves 6-8

Recipe: <u>Date Orange Bars</u>

- ½ cup butter
- ½ cup brown sugar
- 1 egg
- 1 tsp grated orange peel
- 1 cup all-purpose flour
- ½ tsp baking powder
- ½ tsp baking soda
- ¼ cup milk
- ¼ cup orange juice
- ½ cup walnuts, chopped
- ½ cup dates, chopped

Cream butter and brown sugar until fluffy. Add egg and orange peel. Mix well. Sift together flour, baking powder and soda into mixture. Stir well. Add liquids, nuts and dates and mix well. Spread in 11"x7"x1½" pan. Bake at 350F degrees for 25 minutes. Cool. Sprinkle with confectioners' sugar. Enjoy!

Makes 24

Recipe: <u>Cry Baby Cookies</u>

- 1 egg
- 1 cup molasses
- 1 cup sugar
- 1 cup milk
- 2/3 cup butter
- ½ tsp cloves
- ½ tsp cinnamon
- 5 cups flour
- 2 tsp baking soda

Mix well. Drop on greased pan from teaspoon. Bake in 400F degree oven for 8-10 minutes or until golden brown. Enjoy!

Recipe: <u>Cocoa Meringues</u>

- 4 egg whites
- 1/8 tsp salt
- 1 lb confectioners' sugar
- 2 tsp vanilla
- ¾ cup cocoa
- 1 cup chocolate chips

Beat egg whites and salt in bowl with mixer, until foamy. Gradually add sugar and turn to high speed. Beat until mixture forms soft peaks (may take a while). Beat in vanilla and cocoa then add chocolate chips. Drop on greased cookie sheet. Bake at 325F degrees for 10 minutes. Top should be firm but inside should be soft. Cool and remove carefully from pan. These are for chocolate lovers! Enjoy!

SWEETS AND TREATS

Recipe: <u>Good Chocolate Fudge Sauce</u>

- 3 squares unsweetened chocolate
- ¼ cup water
- 1 cup sugar
- 3 tbs white karo syrup
- 1 cup evaporated milk
- 1 tsp vanilla

Melt chocolate in double boiler. Add water slowly, stirring until smooth. Add sugar and karo syrup. Boil until it forms a soft ball in cold water or 234F degrees. Add milk and vanilla. Keeps a long time in refrigerator. Enjoy!

Recipe: <u>Hot Fudge Sauce</u>

- 2 squares unsweetened chocolate
- ½ cup butter
- 2 cups confectioners' sugar, sifted
- ¾ cup evaporated milk

Slowly melt butter and chocolate in sauce pan. Remove from fire and add sugar and evaporated milk alternately. Stir until smooth. Return to fire and simmer 8-10 minutes. Enjoy!

Makes 2 cups

Recipe: <u>Peanut Butter Fudge</u>

- 3 cups brown sugar
- ¾ cup milk
- salt, dash

When this is cooked, add peanut butter the size of a walnut. Enjoy!

Recipe: <u>Caramels</u>

- 2 cups sugar
- 1 ½ cups dark Karo
- 2 cups heavy cream
- 1 cup butter
- 4 squares baking chocolate
- 2 tsp vanilla
- 1 cup chopped nut meats
- 1 cup cream

Boil sugar and Karo, butter and cream up hard. Then add rest of cream. Boil to hard ball stage or 240F degrees. Remove from heat. Add vanilla and nuts and stir in chocolate until melted. Pour into 9x13" pan and let harden. Cut and wrap in waxed paper. Enjoy!

Recipe: <u>Nut and Fruit Confections</u>

- 1 lb figs
- 1 lb dates
- 1 lb English walnuts

Remove stems from figs. Remove stones from dates. Mix with walnuts. Force all through meat chopper. Using a knead board, sprinkle confectioners' sugar instead of flour. Roll about ¼ inch thick and cut into shape. Enjoy!

Recipe: <u>Spiced Sugared Nuts</u>

- 1 cup sugar
- 5 tbs water
- 1 tbs cinnamon
- 1 tsp vanilla
- 1 ¾ cups pecans or walnuts

Boil sugar, water, cinnamon and vanilla. Add nuts. Cook 2 minutes. Remove from fire and stir gently with wooden spoon until mixture hardens. Pour onto buttered platter and separate nuts. Enjoy!

Recipe: <u>Cocoa Meringues</u>

- 4 egg whites
- 1/3 tsp salt
- 1 lb confectioners' sugar
- 2 tsp vanilla
- ¾ cup cocoa
- 1 cup chocolate chips

Beat egg whites salt in bowl with mixer until foamy. Gradually add sugar and turn to hi speed. Beat until mixture forms soft peaks. Beat in vanilla and cocoa, add chocolate chips.

www.ingramcontent.com/pod-product-compliance
Lightning Source LLC
Chambersburg PA
CBHW080523030726
47592CB00012B/3455